Spiritual Shades

Kristin McLeod

BookLeaf
Publishing

Presentation by *BookLeaf Publishing*

Web: www.bookleafpub.com

E-mail: info@bookleafpub.com

ISBN: 9789358735673

First edition 2023

*For all who have or are walking on this
Spiritual path with me.*

ACKNOWLEDGEMENT

Acknowledging the gift of promise found in every spectrum and walk of life.

PREFACE

The Spiritual promise of every rainbow packaged in the lives of historical women.

Worship in Heaven

God's lasting promise
Putting a bow in the clouds
For all living things

Spirited spectrum
Of God's never-ending light
Touching all our lives

In front of the throne
Seven lighted torches burn
God's lasting promise

Eve

Garden of Eden gleaming with colors we could
only imagine.
Entrusted with the stewardship over the land.
Nestled in the paradise of trees bursting with
knowledge.
Illuminating God's own image
Succumbing to the subtle serpent's secretive
suggestions
Inheritance of this original sin handed down.
Sending forth tales of what is good and what is
bad.

Nature's Almanac

The production of the grape
A testimony of climatic variations
The story of the year as impacted by
environmental factors.
Tree rings chronicling the draught or abundance
or water.

Sacred Vows

4

Love comes in many words.
Agape
Phileo
Storge
Eros
Ours was the first proclamation of marital love.
Completely sincere
Warm

Grape harvest

5

Marsanne
Golden straw color
asian pear mandarin orange
tantalizing scent

Counoise
Deeply versatile
complexity and focus
let it rest to peak

Syrah
Deep, dark inkiness
elegant berry bouquet
purple and black fruits

Destiny
Will dry your mouth out
before hitting it again
with lush full body

Varietal
Beautifully balanced
loaded blend for rich palates
complex elegence

Malbec
Mister popular
decadent plush density
forward and showy

Lair of loneliness

The cursed sea urchin
winds below the deep waters
imperial ink

Dreaming of the skins
Maklak, polar bear and seal
Things foreign to here

This was a land of
disgraceful denigration
forgotten peoples

Hoarded, hidden tales
A cavern of denied truths
Deeper than the sea

Treasure

Dutch, buff, orpiment
a deep reddish orange goldfish
marigold seed pods

Breathing forth the dreams
Of pirates sailing the seas
in search of treasure

Twinkling of jewels
buried far within the land
just outside of reach

Mary Magdelene

Seven demons
Respond to the desires of men
Offering bodies up in sin
Youthful ignorance
Guilty of forbidden acts
Blessed with the forgiveness of Christ
Immortal prayers of abundant baptism
Virtuous once again

Venus

Aphrodite's pangs bring both heartache and
delight.
Spewing forth passion and spiritual love
The dual-nature wield
Affections given to the faithful,
Romance in the air at evening
The warlike passion returns in the morning
while the
Evening star's bright spark gleaming in the
deepening dusk

The only

To be the only female
Judge on the court that tried Jesus

To be the only female
Teacher in the school that taught Einstein

To be the only female
Doctor in the hospital that treated traitors

To be the only female
Leader in the land that killed the rights of
women

To be the only female
That stands in the adversity of men.

Delilah

12

I think of power
Through history and honor
Must learn from our past

Liberty's price tag
Too many memorials
The cost of freedom

Od

13

The mysterious
disappearance of Odur
sprung forth Freya's tears

Golden streams of loss
Kisses he had forgotten
Still fresh on her lips

Cork

Celebration time
The sound of a champagne pop
Happiness Abounds

Baptism

15

Wisdom passed through cells
much like everything else.

Restoration through the waters
of forgiveness that brings us back to him.

Spring Category

The deepness of herbs
grown in a shallow soil
a fantastic franc

Silky carmenere
unmistakable pepper note
exclusivity

Mutated noir
delicately refreshing
alsace inspired

The Visitation

God's Invitation
Honor of saying yes
Shared between women

Gabriel graced the Earth with news from afar.
Sixth months apart, but with the same message

Fearing she was too old.
Fearing she was too young.

Filled with the Holy Spirit
Pregnant with the Son of God

The child in my womb leapt for joy
The prophesy fulfilled.

The Lord's power upon both children
The most blessed of all women.

Handed down

All our grandfathers
generational secrets
spilled in the battle

All our grandmothers
generational healing
found during the war

To accept guidance
generational repair
ancestral trauma

Teetering

Sunrise and sunset
Balance in opposition
Sacred partnerships

The night and the day
Are more alike than we think
As are dark and light

A sunlit serpent
slithering through the shadows
not always evil

Things aren't as they seem
always give a second glance
and a second chance

The 19th

Women's right to vote
decades of agitation
protested vict'ry

Efforts of women
It is about the children
political rights

Women and children
intertwining cords once cut
but never severed.